D0852429

anythink

Project

Earth

THE PROJECT
MAKERS

Camilla de la Bédoyère

WINDMILL
BOOKS

Published in 2020 by Windmill Books,
an imprint of Rosen Publishing
29 East 21st Street, New York, NY 10010

Copyright © 2020 Miles Kelly Publishing

Publishing Director: Belinda Gallagher
Creative Director: Jo Cowan
Senior Editor: Fran Bromage
Senior Designer: Rob Hale
Consultant: Anne Rooney
Indexer: Marie Lorimer
Image Manager: Liberty Newton
Production: Elizabeth Collins, Jennifer Brunwin-Jones
Reprographics: Stephan Davis
Assets: Lorraine King

Cataloging-in-Publication Data

Names: de la Bédoyère, Camilla.
Title: Project Earth / Camilla de la Bédoyère.
Description: New York : Windmill Books, 2020. | Series: The project makers
| Includes index.
Identifiers: ISBN 9781538392317 (pbk.) | ISBN 9781725393059 (library bound)
| ISBN 9781538392324 (6 pack)
Subjects: LCSH: Earth science projects--Juvenile literature. | Earth sciences--
Experiments--Juvenile literature. | Science projects--Juvenile literature.

Classification: LCC QE29.D445 2019 | DDC 550.78--dc23

Manufactured in the United States of America

CPSIA Compliance Information: Batch #BW20WM:
For Further Information contact Rosen Publishing,
New York, New York at 1-800-237-9932

How to use the projects

This book is packed full of amazing facts about the Earth. There are also 11 cool projects, designed to make the subject come alive.

Before you start a project:

- Always ask an adult to help you.
- Read the instructions carefully.
- Gather all the supplies you need.
- Clear a surface to work on and cover it with newspaper.

- Wear an apron or old T-shirt to protect your clothing.

Notes for helpers:

- Children will need supervision for the projects, usually because they require the use of scissors, or preparation beforehand.
- Read the instructions together before starting and help to gather the equipment.

IMPORTANT NOTICE
The publisher and author cannot be held responsible for any injuries, damage, or loss resulting from the use or misuse of any of the information in this book.

SAFETY FIRST!
Be careful when using glue or anything sharp, such as scissors.

How to use:
If your project doesn't work the first time, try again — just have fun!

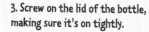

Tornado in a bottle

Supplies:
The equipment should be easy to find, around the house or from a craft store. Always ask before using materials from home.

Numbered stages:
Each stage of the project is numbered and the illustrations will help you. Follow the stages in the order shown to complete the project. If glue or paint is used, make sure it is dry before moving on to the next stage.

Explore the way that liquids spin. Spinning air works the same way to create tornadoes.

SUPPLIES

water • jug • clear plastic bottle with lid • glitter • dishwashing liquid

HOW TO MAKE

1. Using a jug, fill the plastic bottle with water until it's half full.

2. Add a few drops of dishwashing liquid and sprinkle in a few pinches of glitter.

3. Screw on the lid of the bottle, making sure it's on tightly.

4. Turn the bottle upside down and hold it by the neck. Spin the bottle in a circular motion so the water swirls around inside.

5. Stop and watch your mini tornado forming in the water!

WHAT, HOW, WHY?

The whirling funnel shape you can see is called a vortex. When moving air (wind) gets energy from the Sun and warms up, it can also make a vortex.

CONTENTS

THE LIVING PLANET 4
Big Bang 5
DYNAMIC EARTH 6
Chocolate planet 7
EXPLOSIVE ERUPTIONS 8
Make a mudflow 9
RATTLE AND ROLL 10
Make a seismometer 11
WATER WORLD 12
Disappearing act 13
EARLY LIFE 14
BIOMES 16
THE WATER CYCLE 20
Make a mini water cycle 20

AIR AND ATMOSPHERE 22
Lightning strikes 23
EXTREME WEATHER 24
Tornado in a bottle 24
EARTH'S RESOURCES 26
Rock cakes 27
POWERING THE PLANET 28
Potato power! 29
REDUCE, REUSE, RECYCLE 30
"Help the Earth" picture 30
INDEX AND ACKNOWLEDGMENTS 32

THE LIVING PLANET

Planet Earth is a tiny spinning rock in a vast universe, but we call it home. It is the only place we know about that can support life, because it has an atmosphere, water, land, and just the right amount of light and heat from the Sun.

The Sun is a vast ball of hydrogen and helium that works like a nuclear reactor to make energy as light and heat.

COMFORT BLANKET

There is a thick blanket of invisible gases around the Earth (including oxygen, nitrogen, and carbon dioxide). This is called the atmosphere. It keeps the planet warm and protects it from the Sun's radiation – a powerful, burning energy.

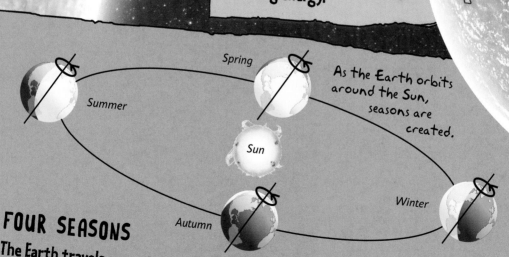

Summer

Spring

Sun

Autumn

Winter

As the Earth orbits around the Sun, seasons are created.

FOUR SEASONS

The Earth travels around the Sun once every 365 days, which gives us a year. Our planet is tilted, and the north and south halves take turns to lean toward the Sun for a time and get more heat and light. That time, or season, is called summer. It's colder and darker in places that tilt away from the Sun, so they experience winter.

Big Bang

Scientists believe the universe began with a giant explosion called the Big Bang. Try this fun experiment to make a big bang of your own.

SUPPLIES

paper towel • tablespoon • small cup • white vinegar • small plastic bag that zips shut • baking soda • warm water

HOW TO MAKE

1. Put a tablespoon of baking soda in the middle of a paper towel and twist the paper towel to make a small packet.

2. Pour half a cup of vinegar into the plastic bag, and add a quarter of a cup of warm water.

3. Zip the bag shut, leaving a gap just big enough for the baking soda packet.

4. Carefully push the packet into the bag, but try to keep it out of the liquid while you zip the bag shut.

5. As you put the bag on the ground, give it a bit of a shake and stand well back.

6. Wait and watch what happens!

WHAT, HOW, WHY?

You will use vinegar (an acid) to release carbon dioxide from baking soda. The gas will be trapped in a bag, until the bag rips open under pressure and creates a mini-explosion.

LIFE ON EARTH

At first, Earth was far too hot for life. As it cooled, the atmosphere and oceans formed and life began to develop. Now there is a huge range of life, from tiny bacteria to millions of animals and plants.

Time line

13.7 BILLION YEARS AGO (BYA)
The Big Bang occured, creating the universe.

4.6 BYA
A cloud of gas and dust cooled to become our Sun and its planets – the solar system.

4.5 BYA
A rocky planet the size of Mars crashed into Earth and created the Moon.

4–3.5 BYA
The first signs of life on Earth appeared.

2.4 BYA
Oxygen appeared in the atmosphere, which all plants and animals need.

DYNAMIC EARTH

The land beneath your feet feels solid and still, but it is moving – very slowly! The Earth is covered in a rocky layer called the crust, with Earth's continents and oceans sitting on large pieces of this crust. These pieces, or plates, move because of liquid rock beneath them.

Two plates meet in the middle of the Atlantic Ocean, at the Mid-Atlantic Ridge.

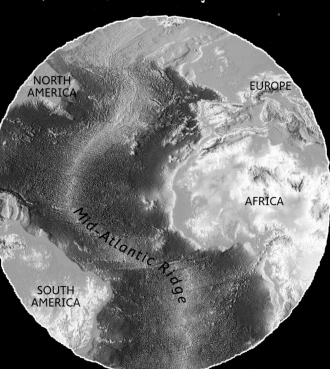

NORTH AMERICA

EUROPE

AFRICA

Mid-Atlantic Ridge

SOUTH AMERICA

MOVING PLATES
The large areas of rocky crust covering the Earth are broken up into giant pieces like a jigsaw puzzle. The moving plates cause continental drift – the way land moves over long periods of time.

ATLANTIC OCEAN

GROW ZONE
When hot rock rises in the mantle, it can force two plates apart. At the Mid-Atlantic Ridge, new rock is added to the plate edges. This makes the ocean floor bigger and pushes the continents further apart.

As rising rock forces the plates apart, a ridge is created. This is called a divergent boundary.

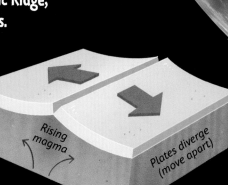

Rising magma

Plates diverge (move apart)

Chocolate planet

Discover how Earth's hot core makes the mantle move, creating convection currents and moving the crust.

SUPPLIES
small saucepan (a glass one is best so you can see the convection currents from the side) • hot chocolate powder • milk

WHAT TO DO
1. Pour cold milk into a pan until it is about two-thirds full. The milk represents the mantle.

2. Shake the chocolate powder carefully over the surface to create the Earth's crust.

3. Ask an adult to help you gently heat the pan. If your pan has glass sides, you will see the "mantle" moving with convection currents. Then you will see it begin to bubble up and break through the "crust."

After you have finished the experiment, you can stir the chocolate powder into the milk to create a delicious hot drink!

INNER CORE
State: solid
Thickness: 746 miles (1,200 km)
Temperature: 9,032–12,630° F (5,000–7,000°C)

OUTER CORE
State: liquid
Thickness: 1,367 miles (2,200 km)
Temperature: up to 9,032°F (5,000°C)

If you could look inside the Earth, you'd see three layers: core, mantle, and crust.

MANTLE
State: solid
Thickness: 1,864 miles (3,000 km)
Temperature: up to 6,330°F (3,500°C)

CRUST
State: solid
Thickness: up to 31 miles (50 km)
Temperature: up to 1,830°F (1,000°C)

On the move

Today there are **seven major plates** and many smaller ones.

They move at a rate of up to 4 inches (10 cm) a year.

As the crust moves away from a **divergent zone**, it cools.

At the edge of the ocean, the **ocean crust** sinks under the edge of the continental crust and melts.

Scientists are still trying to work out exactly how and why

TRANSFORM
A transform fault is a place where two plates slide past one another. The plates are not created or destroyed, they just move.

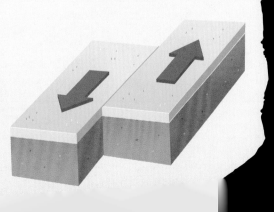

EXPLOSIVE ERUPTIONS

When a volcano erupts, there may be rivers of scorching liquid rock, clouds of toxic ash, or even giant rock-bombs raining down from the skies. This is one of the planet's most incredible, natural, and deadly events — and a sign that Earth's fiery interior is on the move.

INSIDE A VOLCANO

As layers of lava (1) erupt they build up into layers (2) that create a cone-shaped volcano. A chamber beneath the volcano holds a pool of magma (3) and the channels through which the magma flows are called vents (4).

HOT ROCK

Melted rock in the Earth's mantle is called magma. Where the crust is thin and pressure builds up, magma can break through and pour out, erupting as lava.

VOLCANIC STATES

Active = erupting
Dormant = between eruptions
Extinct = not expected to erupt again

Famous volcanoes

AD 79 Mount Vesuvius

Rock, ash and toxic gas destroyed the Roman towns of Pompeii and Herculaneum.

1815 Mount Tambora

This massive volcano exploded in Indonesia, causing tsunamis. Clouds of ash changed the world's climate, causing famine and war.

INSTANT IMPACT

A volcanic eruption can immediately affect the lives of people nearby, but its effects may be felt much further away. Clouds of dust and ash may spread all over the world, blocking out sunlight and changing the weather for years afterwards.

Fountains and rivers of red-hot lava erupt from a shield volcano in Hawaii.

TYPES AND SHAPES

Mountain-shaped volcanoes are called cone volcanoes, and they are found on land and under the sea. Other types are broader and flatter, so they are called shield volcanoes.

This volcano on the island of Luzon in the Philippines is one of the most perfect examples of a cone volcano.

Make a mudflow

After flash floods, mudflows are common on mountains and volcanoes. The way the mud moves is strange because, combined with water, it can flow freely, or become suddenly very gloopy. It's called a non-Newtonian fluid and you can make your own version. Prepare to be amazed!

SUPPLIES

water • cup • wooden spoon
• cornstarch • deep bowl or container

WHAT TO DO

Pour a cup of cornstarch into the container. Add half a cup of water and mix it up.

Experiment with the mixture by:

- grabbing a handful of the mixture and squeezing it
- sticking the end of the wooden spoon in it
- stirring it slowly, then quickly

Can you work out what actions make it liquid-like, and what makes it suddenly go solid?

1883 Krakatoa
The volcanic island of Krakatoa was almost blown apart by a massive eruption, causing a huge loss of life.

1902 Mount Pelée
An eruption on the island of Martinique wiped out the city of St Pierre with winds at more than 1,830°F (1,000°C).

1991 Mount Pinatubo
Millions of tons of magma and toxic gases polluted the atmosphere, reducing the world's temperature for several years.

RATTLE AND ROLL

Huge amounts of energy are released when plates move suddenly. Solid rock trembles and shudders, causing tiny tremors to enormous earthquakes, which can sometimes have dreadful effects.

About 9,000 people died and 3.5 million lost their homes during the 2015 earthquake in Nepal.

Nepal, where The Gorkha Earthquake occurred

Eurasian plate

Arabian plate

Indian plate

Philippine plate

African plate

Indo-Australian plate

Antarctic plate

EARTHQUAKES

Most earthquakes occur at the edges of tectonic plates. As the plates move they may get stuck, until a sudden release of pressure allows a big movement that causes tremors, or shakes.

How big?

The size of an earthquake is recorded using equipment called a seismometer, and measured using the Moment Magnitude Scale. It starts at 1 and can go up to 10 or above.

2 you might notice some shaking
4 objects fall off shelves, little damage
6 shaking felt far away, damage to buildings
8 major damage, buildings collapse
10 total or near-total destruction

FOCUS!

Where an earthquake begins, deep underground, is called its focus. The epicenter is the point on the Earth's surface directly above the focus. Thousands of earthquakes occur every year, but most are Magnitude 2 or less.

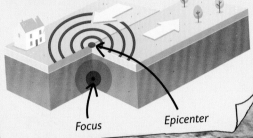

Focus   Epicenter

A tsunami can sweep over land with strength and speed, destroying everything in its way.

NATURAL DISASTER

In 2004, one of the world's biggest recorded earthquakes occurred in the Indian Ocean. The giant tsunami hit land in 15 countries, with waves that reached 65.6 feet (20 m) in height. It became one of the worst natural disasters ever witnessed.

Make a seismometer

What happens to the line when you tap the box with more force?

Follow these steps to make a simple seismometer and measure movement.

SUPPLIES

cardboard box • scissors • plastic cup • marker • sticky tack • string • small stones • paper

HOW TO MAKE

1. Cut the flaps off the box and lie it on its side. Carefully make two small holes in the top.

2. Lay a piece of paper in the bottom of the box.

3. Cut a small hole in the base of the cup for the marker to fit into, and two holes on opposite sides of the rim.

4. Secure the marker (point side out) with sticky tack.

5. Half fill the cup with stones to weigh it down.

6. Run string through the other two holes in the cup, and through the holes in the box, so the cup hangs down.

7. Hold the string so the marker touches the paper and, once it's in the right position, tie the string.

8. Now try tapping the box gently, while pulling the paper towards you. The marker creates a recording of the movement.

4

7

11

WATER WORLD

Seen from space, Earth is a blue planet with swirling white clouds, thanks to the huge amount of water it holds. It is because of this water that there is life, and most living things exist in the oceans.

Coral reefs grow in shallow water. They need sunlight and water that is warm and clean.

ON THE MOVE

Water in the ocean is always on the move. Wind and warmth together whip up the surface water, creating waves. The oceans have currents flowing in huge circles called gyres. Cool water flows closer to the seabed.

A skilled surfer can balance on the crest of a wave. It's a thrilling ride to shore!

OCEAN POTION

Ocean water contains many dissolved gases and salts, as well as tiny animals and plants. It's home to more life than any other habitat on Earth, from blue whales (the largest animals to ever live) to the thumb-sized krill they eat.

EXTREME OCEAN

Surfers make the most of giant waves, but oceans can be dangerous. When two waves crash into each other they can create a rogue wave, which at more than 33 feet (10 m) tall can sink a ship. Unusually high tides may flood towns and villages.

Disappearing act

Salt dissolves in water, which means you can't see it, but it is still there. Prove this for yourself with a simple experiment.

SUPPLIES

glass measuring cup • dessert spoon • hot water • table salt • clean baking tray with edges

WHAT TO DO

1. Pour two heaped dessert spoons of salt into 1 cup (250 ml) of hot water in the measuring cup.

2. Notice how the water turns cloudy, but soon begins to turn clear.

3. Stir the mixture until it turns completely clear.

4. You've now made a solution of salt and water (it's called a solution because the salt has dissolved).

5. Carefully pour the solution into the clean baking tray and leave it to dry, perhaps outside in the sun or near a radiator. For a faster result, you can put the baking tray in the oven, on a low heat, until the water is all gone.

WHAT, HOW, WHY?

As the solution warms up, the water evaporates (turns from a liquid to water vapor, which is a gas). There is no water to keep the salt dissolved, so it returns to being solid crystals of salt.

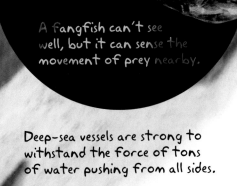

A fangfish can't see well, but it can sense the movement of prey nearby.

Deep-sea vessels are strong to withstand the force of tons of water pushing from all sides.

The five oceans

PACIFIC OCEAN

The **largest** ocean, covering more than 62 million square miles (160 million square km), with twice as much water as the next largest ocean, the Atlantic.

ATLANTIC OCEAN

A giant spreading rift runs down the middle and marks where the Atlantic is **growing**.

INDIAN OCEAN

The **warmest** of the three biggest oceans.

ARCTIC OCEAN

The **smallest** ocean is around the North Pole and partly covered in ice all year.

SOUTHERN OCEAN

This ocean surrounds **Antarctica**.

EARLY LIFE

No one knows what turned Earth from a hot, steamy space rock into a lush, green planet of life. All we do know is that 3.5 billion years ago tiny bacteria – a simple form of life – already existed. They appeared at about the same time the oceans formed.

ALL CHANGE

Since those early days in Earth's history, life has flourished and there are now billions of living things, and many millions of species – most of them are still waiting to be discovered.

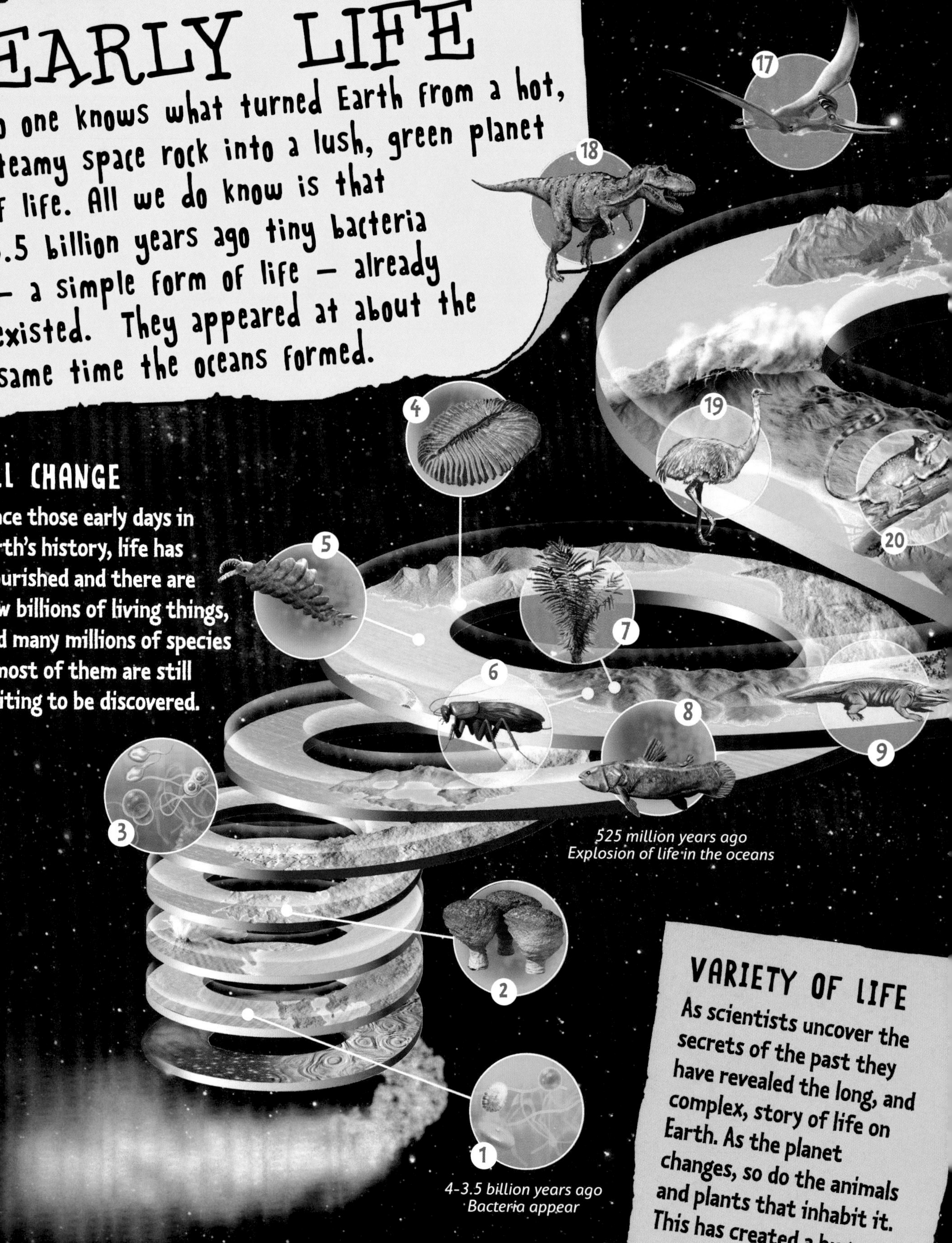

525 million years ago
Explosion of life in the oceans

4-3.5 billion years ago
Bacteria appear

VARIETY OF LIFE

As scientists uncover the secrets of the past they have revealed the long, and complex, story of life on Earth. As the planet changes, so do the animals and plants that inhabit it. This has created a huge variety of life-forms.

This diagram shows the evolution of life, from the very first organisms that appeared more than 3 billion years ago to modern humans.

150-190 million years ago
First flowering plants

230-210 million years ago
First dinosaurs and mammals appear

150 million years ago
First birds appear

EVOLUTION

The way that living things adapt and change over time is called evolution. Living things that do not evolve eventually die out – this is extinction.

The last dodo was seen in 1662. Humans caused its extinction.

Evolution through time key

1 Simple cells
2 Cyanobacteria
3 Cnidarians (soft-bodied animals)
4 Dickinsonia (early marine animal)
5 *Anomalocaris* (arthropod – animals with segmented bodies and no backbone)
6 Cockroach (insect)
7 Cycad (cone-bearing plant)
8 Coelacanth (fish)
9 *Diadectes* (reptile-like amphibian)
10 *Dimetrodon* (mammal-like reptile)
11 Plesiosaur (marine reptile)
12 *Liliensternus* (dinosaur)
13 Pterosaur (flying reptile)
14 Brachiosaur (large dinosaur)
15 Magnolia (flowering plant)
16 *Archaeopteryx* (early bird)
17 *Quetzalcoatlus* (pterosaur – flying reptile)
18 *Tyrannosaurus rex* (dinosaur)
19 Moa (flightless bird)
20 *Plesiadapis* (mammal)
21 *Paracetherium* (rhinoceros-like mammal)
22 *Smilodon* (carnivorous mammal)
23 *Macrauchenia* (hoofed mammal)
24 Wolf (carnivorous mammal)
25 *Homo sapiens* (modern human)

BIOMES

Lions live in dry grasslands and alligators live in lush wetlands. The places that animals and plants live are called their habitats. The particular environment and the animals and plants in it form a biome.

Herds of African elephants live on the savanna.

A polar bear's habitat includes land, ice, and seawater.

GRASSLAND

Grasslands have less water all year round than forests, but are wetter than deserts. In Africa, grassland is called savanna, but in other parts of the world grassland is known as prairie, pampas, or steppe.

POLAR

The winter is long and cold in a polar biome and the land is covered in ice for most, or all, of the year.

What is a biome?

A biome is a population of animals and plants in a particular type of **environment**.

Each biome has a particular type of **climate** (weather patterns), soil, and wetness.

The **animals** and **plants** of a biome are suited to the conditions of their environment.

Amphibians, such as frogs and salamanders, need wet habitats.

Koalas live in dry forests of gum trees.

TEMPERATE

Temperate places rarely experience extreme weather and there are four seasons. Woodland and conifer forests are examples of temperate biomes.

DESERT

Rain rarely falls in a desert, making this one of the most challenging environments for plant and animal life.

Desert snakes can survive a long time without food or water.

The Arabian oryx is adapted for life in the desert. However, it has been hunted and is now rare.

The pattern and color of this snow leopard's fur helps it hide in its habitat.

MOUNTAIN

The habitats at the foot of the mountain are very different from those at the top, where it is often cold and dry. Few trees can grow high on a mountain.

TROPICAL FOREST

Rainy days and strong sunshine all year make tropical forests a superb habitat for millions of plants and animals.

A huge beak helps this toucan reach the juiciest fruit at the tip of the branches.

Leafcutter ants build giant nests underground.

Crocodiles are superb swimmers, but they can run fast, too.

Thick, soft feathers keep a snowy owl warm.

TUNDRA

Cold, bleak, and treeless plains between the Arctic and temperate forests form the tundra biome. Below the soil, the ground is permanently frozen.

FRESHWATER

Rivers, lakes, and ponds are home to fish and many invertebrates. Other animals come to the water to drink, or catch prey.

Coral reefs make a perfect habitat for many ocean animals.

OCEAN

The largest, most mysterious of all Earth's biomes, the oceans contain the smallest and largest animals on the planet.

THE WATER CYCLE

The amount of water on the planet and in its atmosphere stays the same, but it is always on the move between the land, the oceans, and the air. The way that water moves around the Earth is called the water cycle.

WATERY PLANET

Water exists on Earth in three different states, depending on its temperature: solid (ice), liquid (water), and gas (water vapor).

Sunlight warms the oceans and water evaporates. It rises into the sky.

Make a mini water cycle

Create a mini water cycle to watch how water can turn from a liquid to a gas and back again.

SUPPLIES

large plastic bowl • small mug • plastic wrap • cold water • jug

WHAT TO DO

1. Place a clean, dry mug in the middle of the bowl. Make sure the edges of the bowl are taller than the mug.

2. Carefully pour cold water into the bowl (but not inside the mug) until it is about 2/3 full of water. The water represents the ocean and the mug is like a mountain on land.

❷

3. Cover the bowl with plastic wrap. Make sure it is tightly sealed around the edge of the bowl.

4. Leave the bowl somewhere warm (in the sun or by a radiator). The time you will need to leave the bowl depends on the temperature.

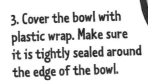
❹

WHAT, HOW, WHY?

Heat gives the water the energy it needs to turn into an invisible vapor – it evaporates. The vapor cools when it touches the plastic wrap and turns back into a liquid – it condenses. Water droplets appear on the underside of the plastic wrap and start to drip back into the "ocean." Some water will drip into the mug, like rain falling on mountains.

Raging water

The Colorado River has eroded through 1.1 miles (1.8 km) of rock to create the **Grand Canyon**.

The tallest waterfall in the world is **Angel Falls** in Venezuela, where water plummets nearly .6 mile (1 km) from a mountaintop!

The mighty Zambezi River tumbles over **Victoria Falls,** which is also known as "the smoke that thunders."

Niagara Falls in North America is the **largest** waterfall by volume of water. Erosion is causing it to move back by about 12 inches (30 cm) every year.

Water vapor creates clouds and wind moves the clouds towards land.

Droplets of water in the clouds get bigger and heavier until they turn to rain or snow over mountains.

Rain, or snow, falls.

As rivers flow from high areas, they move fast and with high energy, eroding the rocks to create valleys.

Frozen rivers of ice occur in regions near the North and South Pole. They are called glaciers.

Rivers with low energy wind across flatter land, creating meanders.

After heavy rain, some water forms floods, flowing over the ground into the rivers or sea. This is called runoff.

Water collects in rivers and flows toward the sea.

At a river mouth, debris is dropped, creating huge fan-shaped areas called deltas.

Rainwater seeping through cracks in rocks can slowly erode the rock away, carving out caves under the ground.

21

AIR AND ATMOSPHERE

As the Sun warms the planet it heats the atmosphere and causes convection currents. They make the air move (creating wind) and carry moisture and heat all around the planet, giving us a world of wonderful weather — from snowstorms to sunny days.

The atmosphere is made up of layers. Beyond it is deep space.

WHAT IS AIR?

Air is the name we give to the collection of gases that make up the bottom layer of the atmosphere. It's where the weather is made. The atmosphere traps warmth, keeping the planet at a steady temperature.

Exosphere   435–6,214 miles

Exosphere – low-level satellites orbit in the two outermost layers of the atmosphere.

Thermosphere   50–435 miles

Thermosphere – the Aurora Borealis can be seen in this layer.

Mesosphere   31–50 miles

Mesosphere – this layer burns up meteorites and asteroids.

Stratosphere   6–31 miles

Troposphere   0–6 miles

Stratosphere – most long-distance aircraft travel in this layer.

Troposphere – weather and clouds occur in the lowest layer.

HAILSTONES

During a hailstorm, solid lumps of ice, called hailstones, fall from the sky. They can be big enough to cause damage and injury!

ELECTRIC SKY

When water or ice crystals in a cloud bump into each other, they make static electricity. If there is enough of it, the cloud charges up like a battery, causing a flash of lightning to zip through the sky. The heat and energy from the lightning make the air expand around it, producing a clap of thunder!

Bolts of electricity fork through the dark sky.

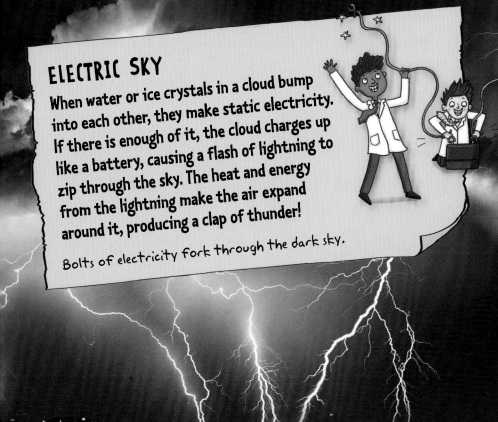

Lightning strikes

A single flash of lightning can release enough energy to power a light bulb for six months. The spark you'll create here is much smaller! Try this experiment on a cool, dry day and turn off the lights to see the flash.

SUPPLIES
tin foil • plastic fork • rubber glove • blown-up balloon • wooden chopping board

WHAT TO DO

1. Fold tin foil around the head of a plastic fork, keeping it flat and smooth.

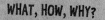

2. Wearing the rubber glove to hold the balloon, rub the balloon over your hair for one minute.

3. Place the balloon on the wooden board.

4. Using your gloved hand, touch the fork to the balloon, so the tin foil is in contact with the surface, and hold it there.

5. Using your bare hand, touch the foil and watch for the flash!

WHAT, HOW, WHY?

Rubbing the balloon on your hair generates static electricity, freeing lots of tiny particles called electrons. They move towards the tin foil, but can't escape until you touch it with your bare finger. The electrons zap across to your skin and down to the ground, creating a flash of electricity.

CIRRUS
Where: high in the sky
Appear: wispy like tufts of hair
Made of: ice crystals
Weather: a change of weather is on the way

ALTOCUMULUS
Where: medium level
Appear: white or gray clumps
Made of: water droplets and ice crystals
Weather: settled and dry

CUMULONIMBUS
Where: from low sky to high in the sky
Appear: large, tall cloud
Made of: ice crystals and water vapor
Weather: rain, possibly thunderstorms

EXTREME WEATHER

Scientists may predict the weather, but there is nothing they can do to control the ever-changing mixture of gases, water, and solar energy that create the weather. Sometimes extreme weather hits the planet with extraordinary, devastating effects.

Snowstorms occur during winter in temperate and polar places.

WHITEOUT

When heavy snow and strong winds work together, they can create terrible blizzards, or snowstorms. In the worst cases, thick blankets of snow cover the ground and dense, falling snow makes it impossible to see your hand in front of your face.

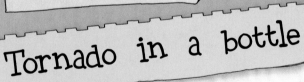

Tornado in a bottle

Explore the way that liquids spin. Spinning air works the same way to create tornadoes.

SUPPLIES
water • jug • clear plastic bottle with lid • glitter • dishwashing liquid

HOW TO MAKE

1. Using a jug, fill the plastic bottle with water until it's half full.

2. Add a few drops of dishwashing liquid and sprinkle in a few pinches of glitter.

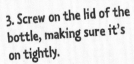

3. Screw on the lid of the bottle, making sure it's on tightly.

4. Turn the bottle upside down and hold it by the neck. Spin the bottle in a circular motion so the water swirls around inside.

5. Stop and watch your mini tornado forming in the water!

WHAT, HOW, WHY?
The whirling funnel shape you can see is called a vortex. When moving air (wind) gets energy from the Sun and warms up, it can also make a vortex.

SANDSTORM

When hot winds scoop up dry sand in the Sahara, they can create violent dust storms, called haboobs. As the giant clouds of sand sweep across the land, they engulf buildings in a dense red mist.

A sandstorm can occur after a time of drought (when there has been no rain).

SPINNING TWISTERS

A twister, or tornado, is a powerful column of air that spins at great speed, causing damage or destruction to anything in its path. Most tornadoes form over land, from a thunderstorm.

A whirling tornado connects a cloud above to the ground below.

Hurricanes and typhoons are enormous spiraling storm clouds that form at sea in warm weather.

Record breakers

HOTTEST TEMPERATURE
134°F (56.7°C)
Death Valley, USA, June 1913

COLDEST TEMPERATURE
−192.6°F (−189.2°C)
Vostok Station, Antarctica, July 1983

MOST RAINY DAYS IN A YEAR
350
Mount Wai'ale'ale, Hawaii

HEAVIEST HAILSTONES
2.2 lbs (1kg)
Bangladesh, India, April 1986

DEEPEST SNOW
39 feet (12 m)
Honshu Island, Japan, 1927

DRIEST PLACE
less than **.03 inch** (.75 mm)
of rain a year,
Atacama Desert, Chile

EARTH'S RESOURCES

Iron, oil, gold, wood, and gas — these are just some of the world's resources that we use every day. Earth provides us with the materials we need to work, learn, build, power our homes, and feed ourselves.

How is it made?

Natural materials

come from animals, plants, or from the ground, like:

Wood Silk
Leather Wool
Oil Iron
Cotton Sand
Gold

Synthetic materials are

man-made, often in factories. Paper is made from wood; plastic is made from oil; glass is made from sand; nylon is made from oil, and steel is made from iron and carbon.

MIGHTY METALS

Metals are very useful materials because they conduct heat and electricity. They are strong but can be molded into different shapes.

At a quarry, stone, slate, gravel, and other resources are removed from the ground.

Cuts are made in the bark of a rubber tree and latex (a thick white liquid) oozes out.

Rubber tree

Bark

Latex

Wire or string

Cup

Rock cakes

Rock cakes, like real rocks, are hard and lumpy. Thankfully they taste much better!

SUPPLIES

mixing bowl • scale • wooden spoon • two forks • knife • baking tray • cooling rack

INGREDIENTS

12 oz (350 g) plain flour • ¼ teaspoon salt • 2 teaspoons baking powder • 6 oz (175 g) light brown sugar • ¼ teaspoon grated nutmeg • ¼ teaspoon pumpkin pie spice • 6 oz (175 g) butter • 4 oz (125 g) mixed fruit • 1 large egg, lightly beaten • 1–2 tablespoons milk

HOW TO MAKE

1. Heat the oven to 375°F (190°C).

As you make the rock cakes, think about where all the things you are using come from, including the fuel that makes the oven hot. If you don't know the answer, use the Internet to do some research.

2. Mix the flour, salt, baking powder, sugar, nutmeg, and pumpkin pie spice in a bowl.

3. Chop up the butter into small slabs and use your fingertips to rub it into the mixture until it looks like breadcrumbs.

4. Stir in the fruit.

5. Add the egg and mix together. Add milk if the mixture is dry.

6. Use two forks to make 10–12 spiky mounds of mixture, evenly spaced on the baking tray.

7. Bake for 18–20 minutes and leave on a cooling rack before eating.

❸

USEFUL ROCKS

A rock is made of minerals, such as quartz, calcite, and salt. Rocks can also contain metals, such as gold and iron, or precious gems like diamonds and emeralds.

FEEDING THE WORLD

Two million years ago, our human ancestors hunted animals and found plants to eat. It was only about 11,500 years ago that early farmers learned how to keep animals and grow their own crops. Today, farming has a bigger impact on the Earth than ever before.

Modern machinery has helped farmers to feed the world.

POWERING THE PLANET

Through human history, wood has been burned for heat and light. Today, we mostly rely on dirty fossil fuels to give us the energy we need to power a modern world. In the future, we will depend on cleaner, sustainable fuels — like solar, wind, and water power.

WHAT ARE FOSSIL FUELS?

Oil, gas, and coal are types of fossil fuels. They were all made millions of years ago from the remains of animals or plants. We take them from the ground, or under the sea, and burn them to generate electricity or fuel homes and vehicles.

A solar panel uses sunlight to make electricity, while a leaf makes chemical energy from it.

A group of wind turbines is called a wind farm.

WIND POWER

One wind turbine can generate enough electricity to power 1,000 homes. They can be built on land or in the sea, but they do need plenty of windy days to be useful.

The upper layer of a leaf is transparent, so more light can pass into it.

The palisade layer is full of chloroplasts. Chloroplasts capture sunlight and turn it into fuel for the plant.

Hot underground water can erupt in a cloud of steam. It is called a geyser.

HOT EARTH

The ground beneath our feet is warm, especially in places where there are hot springs or tectonic activity. That heat can be used as a source of energy. It's called geothermal energy.

Potato power!

Electric cars are becoming more popular because they use power stored in batteries instead of burning a fossil fuel. Make your own potato battery to power a clock.

SUPPLIES
- 2 big potatoes • 2 large galvanized nails
- 2 lengths of copper wire 1 inch (2 cm) long
- 3 alligator clips with leads • battery clock

WHAT TO DO
1. Remove the battery from the clock.

2. Label the potatoes "1" and "2." This will help you attach the clips correctly later.

3. Push one galvanized nail halfway into an end of each potato.

4. Stick a piece of copper wire halfway into the other end of each potato. (The wire and the nail should not touch each other.)

5. Follow the diagram below to attach two alligator clips to the potatoes and the battery terminals in the clock.

6. Use the third alligator clip to join the two potatoes.

7. Your clock should start working again!

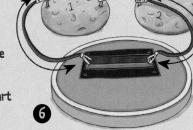

WHAT, HOW, WHY?
The potato conducts electricity between the two nails. The inside of a potato is acidic. The acid makes electrons leave the zinc nail and travel through the potato to the copper wire, creating an electric current, in just the same way that a battery does.

What is energy?

Energy is the **ability to do work**, or make things happen.

Energy can't be made or destroyed, but it can be **changed** from one type to another. Heat, light, and electricity are three types of energy.

We get **light** and **heat** from the Sun's energy, but we also get energy from fuels such as oil and gas.

REDUCE, REUSE, RECYCLE

Protecting and caring for the Earth is an important job for everyone. There are simple steps we can all take to look after our big, beautiful planet and save its precious resources for the future.

"Help the Earth" picture

Create a picture to help remind people that keeping the world healthy and safe for all living things is a job for everyone.

SUPPLIES

plain paper • dinner plate • map of the world • pencils • pens • paints • glue • scissors

HOW TO MAKE

1. On a plain piece of paper, draw around a large plate to create a circle – this is Earth.

2. Using the map, draw continents on the Earth and color them in green. Color the oceans blue.

3. On another piece of paper, draw around your hands and paint them any color you like.

4. Cut out the Earth and hand shapes.

5. Glue the hands to the back of the Earth so they look as if they are holding the world.

6. On each finger write your ideas for reducing pollution, such as "Walk to school" or "Turn off electric lights."

FOCUS ON POLLUTION

Anything that contaminates, or damages, the natural world is pollution. Everywhere, oceans and coasts have become dirty places because trash, especially plastic, is thrown into rivers or seas. Marine pollution is killing wildlife and damaging habitats around the world.

People are now trying to think of ways to clean up the oceans.

CLIMATE CHANGE

When fossil fuels are burned, they release dangerous gases and chemicals into the air. These greenhouse gases build up in the atmosphere and stop heat from escaping into space. As the world gets warmer and weather patterns change, some animals and plants will strugge to survive.

Plastiki's voyage was powered by wind, and solar panels.

THE FUTURE OF PLASTIC

Environmentalist David de Rothschild created his 59-foot (18 m) boat, Plastiki, from 12,500 plastic bottles and recycled waste. Plastiki sailed from California to Sydney in 2010 to raise awareness of the world's overuse of plastic.

Around the world, people are volunteering their time to clean beaches.

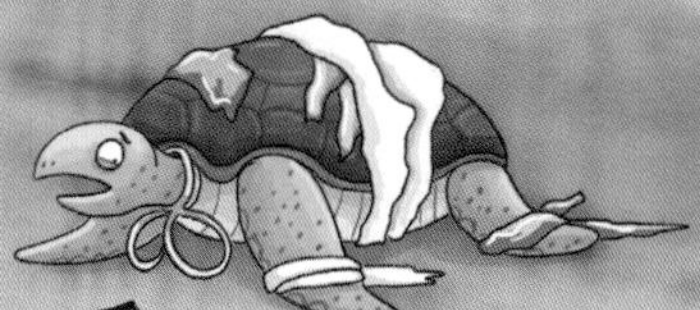

Reduce your eco-footprint by choosing to buy things that aren't wrapped up in lots of unnecessary packaging.

Recycling means turning waste into something we can use again. Glass, plastic, paper, and aluminium can all be recycled.

Find other uses for things you don't need any more, or give them away or sell them.

Here's how long it takes for common trash to break down (decompose):

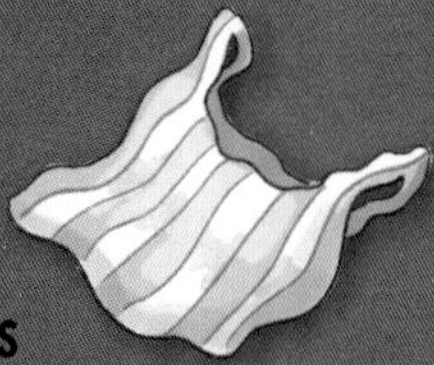

Plastic bag: up to 500 years

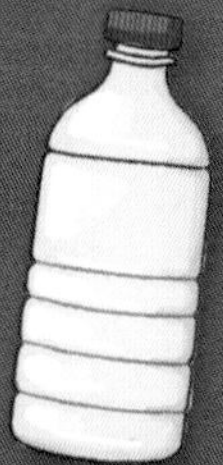

Plastic bottle: up to 450 years

Plastic straw: up to 200 years

Soda can: up to 200 years

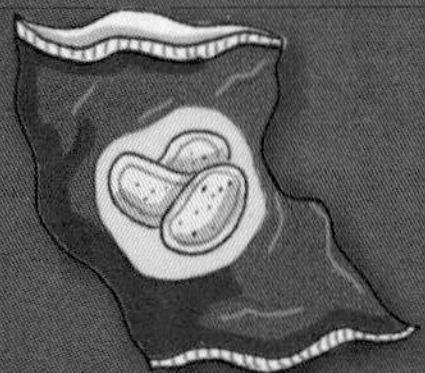

Chip bag: up to 80 years

Cigarette butt: up to 10 years

Apple core: up to 2 months

INDEX

A
air 22
atmosphere 4, 5, 20, 22, 30

B
Big Bang 5
biomes 16–19

C
caring for the Earth 30–31
caves 21
climate change 30
clouds 9, 23
continental drift 6
convection currents 7, 22
coral reefs 12
crust 6, 7

D
deserts 17

E
earthquakes 10–11
electricity 23, 26, 28, 29
energy 4, 20, 23, 28–29
evolution 14, 15

F
farming 27
floods 9, 12, 21, 25
fossil fuels 28, 30
freshwater habitats 19

G
geothermal energy 29
grasslands 16
gravity 5

H
hailstones 22, 25
hurricanes and typhoons 25

L
life on Earth 5, 12, 13, 14–19
lightning 23

M
magma 8
mantle 6, 7, 8
metals 26, 27
Mid-Atlantic Ridge 6
Moon 5
mountains 18, 21
mudflows 9

O
oceans 5, 6, 7, 11, 12–13, 19, 30

P
plate tectonics 6, 7, 10
polar regions 16, 21
pollution 30
potato battery 29

R
radiation 4
rain 17, 21, 22, 25
resources 26–27, 30
rock cakes 27

S
salt water 13
sandstorms 25
seasons 4
seismometers 10, 11
snow 22, 24, 25
solar power 28
solar system 5
storms 24, 25
submersibles 13
Sun 4, 5, 22, 28, 29

T
temperate regions 17
temperatures 25
tides and waves 5, 11, 12
tornadoes 24, 25
tropical forests 18
tsunamis 11
tundra 19

V
volcanoes 8–9

W
water cycle 20–21
waterfalls 21
weather 9, 16, 22, 24–25
wind power 28
winds 22, 24

ACKNOWLEDGMENTS

The publishers would like to thank the following artists who have contributed to this book:

Cover Dan Taylor (The Bright Agency)

Insides Richard Watson (The Bright Agency), Tom Woolley (Astound US Inc)

All other artwork is from the Miles Kelly Artwork Bank

The publishers would like to thank the following sources for the use of their photographs: t = top, c = center, b = bottom, l = left, r = right, bg = background

Getty 30–31(c) Roijoy/iStock; 31(tr) Brendon Thorne/Stringer/Getty Images AsiaPac
NASA 25(bl) UW-Madison/SSEC, William Straka III
Reuters 11(t) Kyodo
Science Photo Library 6(cl) NOAA;
8–9(c) Douglas Peebles; 10(c) Sputnik; 13(b) Sputnik, (br) Dante Fenolio; 14–15(c) Jose Antonio Penas

Shutterstock 2–3(bg), 16–19(bg), 32(bg) iSiripong; 4(bl) Redsapphire; 4–5(c) Aphelleon/NASA; 5(tl) Eric Boucher; 6–7(c) Mopic; 8(cl) VVOE; 9(br) Puripat Lertpunyaroj; 10(cr) Rainer Lesniewski; 12(bl) Vlad61; 12–13(c) EpicStockMedia; 16(tl) Graeme Shannon, (cr) DonLand; 17(tr) Jerry Zitterman, (tl) worldswildlifewonders, (tc) EcoPrint, (bl) Alexander Wong, (br) Kertu; 18(t) Karen Kane, (b) David Evison, (br) Dr Morley Read; 19(tl) Tom Middleton, (tr) Meister Photos, (b) Damsea; 21(br) David A Knight; 22(c) Vadim Sadovski, (b) Kichigin, (bl) Suzanne Tucker; 23(t) Vasin Lee; 24(c) Ipedan; 25(t) BCFC, (bc) Minerva Studio, (b) Leonard Zhukovsky; 26–27(c) Andrey N Bannov; 27(b) Sergey Malov, (br) smereka; 28(c) artjazz; 29(c) Pavel Svoboda Photography
The Seabin Project 31(tr) The Team at Seabin Project

Every effort has been made to acknowledge the source and copyright holder of each picture. Miles Kelly Publishing apologizes for any unintentional errors or omissions.